Guide to Auditor Legal Liability

Steven M. Bragg

AccountingTools®

ISBN 978-1-64221-262-4

For more information about AccountingTools® products, visit our Web site at www.accountingtools.com.

Table of Contents

About the Author

Steven Bragg, CPA, has been the chief financial officer or controller of four companies, as well as a consulting manager at Ernst & Young. He received a master's degree in finance from Bentley College, an MBA from Babson College, and a Bachelor's degree in Economics from the University of Maine. He has been a two-time president of the Colorado Mountain Club, and is an avid alpine skier, mountain biker, and certified master diver. Mr. Bragg resides in Centennial, Colorado. He has written more than 300 books and courses, including *New Controller Guidebook*, *GAAP Guidebook*, and *Payroll Management*.

Steven maintains the accountingtools.com web site, which contains continuing professional education courses, the Accounting Best Practices podcast, and thousands of articles on accounting subjects.

Buy Additional AccountingTools Courses

AccountingTools offers more than 1,500 hours of CPE courses, with concentrations in accounting, auditing, finance, taxation, and ethics. Related courses that you might like include:

- Essentials of Business Law
- Ethical Responsibilities
- How to Conduct an Audit Engagement

Go to accountingtools.com/cpe to view these additional courses.

AccountingTools®

Guide to Auditor Legal Liability

Introduction

Investors and creditors rely upon the auditor's report when examining the financial statements of a business. Given this reliance, it should be no surprise that they will target auditors for redress when they suffer financial losses relating to those businesses, alleging malpractice. Because this risk of lawsuits is always present, auditors need to view *every* audit engagement as one that they may have to defend in court. Even when the plaintiff loses, the cost to defend these cases can be extraordinarily high. Given the risk of lawsuits and the associated defense costs, auditors are required to pay extremely high fees for professional liability insurance. In addition to out-of-pocket costs, auditors also pay for lawsuits in the form of damage to their reputations, which can have severe long-term effects on their ability to acquire clients.

EXAMPLE

Smith & Smith, a CPA firm, audits a small software development company that is working on a promising product that can predict the future purchases of consumers. Its startup capital was provided by a group of limited partners. Smith & Smith audits the firm for three years, charging an average of $35,000 per year for this service. In the fourth year, the client finds that it needs more capital, so it asks the investors for more funds. They refuse, so the client goes bankrupt. The limited partners decide to attempt a recovery of their investment from all possible parties, including the auditors. It is readily apparent that Smith & Smith have conducted their work in accordance with the highest standards, and so cannot realistically be found liable. Nonetheless, they are included in the lawsuit, and so must engage in every phase of the defense process, which costs the firm $500,000. The case is eventually settled in favor of the auditors.

In this situation, the auditors were in no real danger of losing the lawsuit, but still had to incur costs that were nearly five times the aggregate audit fee earned from the engagement.

Auditors are more susceptible to liability claims than other professions, because their work product is relied upon by a much broader cross-section of the population. For example, a plastic surgeon is probably only going to be sued by a dissatisfied patient, while an auditor can potentially be sued by anyone who reads the financial statements of a client. The worst case is when an auditor certifies the financial statements of a publicly-held company, which may have millions of investors – any of whom could bring suit against the auditor. Given the magnitude of the auditor's legal liability, one should always be aware of the nature of this liability and how to mitigate it, as addressed in this manual.

The Reasoning of Plaintiffs

There may be cases in which there was a clear failure by the auditor to address a concern during an audit that would have uncovered a material misstatement in a client's financial statements. In other cases, subsequent events may prove that the financial statements were materially misstated, even though at the time a reasonable person would have considered them to be accurate. For example, consider a situation where a manufacturer of baby strollers has just sold several million units of a new stroller model, and has set aside a reserve for warranty claims that is in line with its history of warranty claims. The auditor agrees with this reserve, and the financial statements are issued. However, a few months later, it becomes apparent that there was a serious flaw in the strollers that triggers an avalanche of lawsuits and warranty claims. Investors in the company suffer major losses as the market value of their shares decline, and decide to recover their losses from the auditor, even if it is not at all clear that the audit firm was at fault. In this case, the investors are looking at a tradeoff of a reasonable chance of generating a payout, against the relatively small cost of filing suit against the auditor. This scenario may not appear fair, but it represents the reality of the auditor's legal situation.

Yet another scenario is when the plaintiff knows that its case is relatively weak, but decides to file suit against the auditor anyways. Its intent is not necessarily to win, but rather to gain an out-of-court settlement from the auditor's insurer in order to make the plaintiff go away. These types of lawsuits can be relatively frequent, and can add up to a substantial amount over time.

Common Law Liability

An auditor can incur a liability through *common law*; this is derived from a history of decisions made in individual cases, usually in the areas of fraud, breach of contract, or negligence. Common law can vary from one state to another, and so can yield different results, depending on the factual circumstances and specific conditions associated with each case. For example:

- *Fraud.* This is a false misrepresentation of the facts, resulting in the object of the fraud receiving an injury by acting upon the misrepresented facts. Thus, a knowing misrepresentation of the facts can result in a lawsuit that alleges fraud. A variation on the concept is *constructive fraud*, which is classified as an unintentional deception or misrepresentation. An auditor can be liable for constructive fraud when the following conditions are present:
    - A false misrepresentation;
    - In reference to a material fact;
    - For the purpose of inducing the other party to rely on such misrepresentation;
    - On which the other party did in fact rely;
    - Which resulted in damages; and
    - Where a fiduciary relationship exists between the parties.

- *Breach of contract.* The auditor promises to perform the services stated in an engagement letter, and then fails to deliver. A liability can arise when the auditor does not perform services and the client suffers monetary damages as a result.
- *Negligence.* The auditor is supposed to exercise a degree of due professional care that is expected of a prudent person under similar circumstances. A failure in this situation is typically caused by a lack of management oversight, inadequate training, or poor judgment, and is known as *ordinary negligence*. For example, when an auditor completes the terms of a contract, but the work contains obvious errors, the client could have a case for alleging ordinary negligence. *Gross negligence* arises when the auditor exhibits a reckless disregard for reasonable care, potentially or actually resulting in losses for the client. For example, a clear failure to follow generally accepted auditing standards in the conduct of an audit would be considered gross negligence. The two concepts differ in the degree of inattention exhibited by the auditor.

When a third party, such as a lender, relies on an auditor's report, the third party can recover losses from the auditor by proving that the losses it incurred were a direct result of the auditor's actions, and that the auditor breached his or her duty of due professional care (as described later). There are three interpretations of the manner in which this liability can be established by a third party, which are:

- *Known user approach.* Under this approach, the auditor can be held liable for ordinary negligence only to the client and any third party that has been specifically identified as a user of the auditor's report. The auditor can still be held liable to unidentified third-party users of the report for gross negligence or fraud. In this case, the report is assumed to have been prepared primarily for the benefit of the client and identified users, which places a larger burden of proof on any plaintiff classified as unidentified.
- *Foreseen user approach.* This approach expands the auditor's liability from the known user approach, where third party users only have to prove ordinary negligence when they are foreseen users of the client's financial statements. For example, when the auditors are informed that the client's financial statements and the auditor's report will be used to obtain financing, a lender who is later approached by the client can be considered a foreseen user, even though the specific lender was not revealed to the auditor. This liability principle is commonly followed in many states.
- *Foreseeable user approach.* This more expansive approach holds that the auditor can be held liable for ordinary negligence to any third party that the auditor may reasonably foresee as being a recipient of the client's financial statements for routine business purposes. This liability principle is rarely followed.

These interpretations are developed from past legal decisions; each variation establishes a different precedent in regard to which parties can hold the auditor liable simply by proving ordinary negligence.

EXAMPLE

An auditor issues an unqualified opinion on the financial statements of a client, where the auditor was aware that her auditor's report would be used by the client to obtain a line of credit from a lender. The client did not identify the specific lender from which it intended to obtain the line of credit. After the auditor released her report, Fourth National Bank relied on it to provide a line of credit to the client. In addition, an investor relied on it to buy a subsidiary from the client.

If the court were to apply the foreseen user approach, the auditor could be held liable to Fourth National if ordinary negligence could be proven. However, the investor would need to prove gross negligence by the auditor to recover its losses, since the audit was not performed to assist in the sale of the client's subsidiary.

Statutory Law Liability

An auditor can also incur a liability through *statutory law*; this is created when a government entity creates laws or regulations that can potentially impose liability on the auditor. For example, statutory liability can arise under federal securities laws, including the following:

Securities Act of 1933

This Act focuses on initial public offerings; it creates a liability for the audit work associated with the initial financial statements produced as part of the initial stock registration effort. The auditor is responsible for making sure that the client's financial statements are fairly stated beyond the date of their issuance, up to the date when the client's *registration statement* becomes effective – which may be a number of months later.

Under the Act, both the entity filing an initial registration statement with the Securities and Exchange Commission (SEC) and its auditors can be found liable by the purchasers of its securities if the registration statement is later found to contain either material misstatements or omissions. The exact wording within the Act that applies to the auditor is contained within Section 11(a), which is as follows:

> (a) ...in case any part of the registration statement... contained an untrue statement of a material fact or omitted to state a material fact required to be stated therein or necessary to make the statements therein not misleading, any person acquiring such security (unless it is proved that at the time of such acquisition he knew of such untruth or omission) may... sue... every accountant... whose profession gives authority to a statement made by him, who has with his consent been

named as having prepared or certified any report or valuation which is used in connection with the registration statement.

Though this statement might appear to establish an all-encompassing liability for the auditor, it really only does so for the initial sale of securities. It offers no protection to all subsequent purchasers of the securities, as they are later sold and resold on a secondary exchange. Nonetheless, for those investors covered by the Act, the burden of proof is largely shifted to the auditor, since the plaintiffs only need to prove that the registration statement was misleading, and that they incurred a loss. There is no provision in the Act that requires a plaintiff to prove that they relied upon the registration statement, or that the auditors were actually negligent in their audit of the client's financial statements.

There are several ways in which an auditor can defend against a plaintiff's allegations under the Act. The options are as follows:

- The audit was conducted with due diligence. Auditors are not liable, as long as they had, after reasonable investigation, reasonable grounds to believe that the statements made in the registration statement were true, and that there were no omissions of material facts. This is the mostly commonly used defense.
- The losses incurred by the plaintiff were not related to the misstated financial statements.
- The plaintiffs knew about the misstated financial statements when they purchased the securities.
- The statute of limitations has expired, which in this case is no more than three years after the securities were first offered to the public.

> **Note:** A secondary purchaser who has purchased securities within the first year of the filing of a registration statement can also bring suit against the auditor under the Act.

When the auditor elects to use the due diligence defense, the court will require that the auditor present a strong proof of innocence, which is why audit firms tend to dig unusually deeply into a client's affairs before they sign off on a registration statement.

Securities Exchange Act of 1934

This Act requires publicly-held companies to file audited annual financial statements with the SEC, as well as reviewed quarterly statements. The Act creates a liability for the audit work associated with these ongoing report filings in relation to anyone who buys or sells the client's securities if the related financial statements are found to be misstated. The exact wording within the Act that applies to the auditor is contained within Sections 10 and 18, which is as follows:

[Section 10] It shall be unlawful for any person to make any untrue statement of a material fact or omit to state any material fact necessary in order to make the statements made, in the light of the circumstances under which they are made, not misleading, or to engage in any fraudulent, deceptive, or manipulative acts or practices, in connection with any tender offer or request or invitation for tenders, or any solicitation of security holders in opposition to or in favor of any such offer, request, or invitation.

[Section 18] …any person (not knowing that such statement was false or misleading) who, in reliance upon such statement shall have purchased or sold a security at a price which was affected by such statement, for damages caused by such reliance, unless the person sued shall prove that he acted in good faith and had no knowledge that such statement was false or misleading. A person seeking to enforce such liability may sue… in any court of competent jurisdiction.

This Act provides protections for not only the original purchasers of securities, but also for subsequent buyers and sellers. To gain a favorable ruling under this Act, plaintiffs must be able to prove that they sustained losses by relying upon the financial statements, and that the financial statements were misleading, where there is an intent to deceive, manipulate, or defraud.

There are several ways in which an auditor can defend against a plaintiff's allegations under the Act. The options are as follows:

- The auditors acted in good faith. This is the most common defense, and can usually be achieved unless the plaintiff can prove the existence of gross negligence or fraud on the part of the auditor.
- The plaintiffs' losses were not related to the auditor's actions.

From the auditor's perspective, the key differences between the 1933 Act and the 1934 Act are as follows:

- The 1933 Act only provides protection to initial purchasers of securities, while the 1934 Act provides protection to subsequent buyers or sellers of securities.
- The 1933 Act does not require plaintiffs to prove reliance upon the audited financial statements, while such reliance is required under the 1934 Act.
- The 1933 Act requires the auditor to prove due diligence, while the 1934 Act requires the auditors to prove that they acted in good faith, while also requiring plaintiffs to prove that the auditor intended to deceive, manipulate, or defraud.

Private Securities Litigation Reform Act

This Act was designed to reduce the number of frivolous securities lawsuits. The Act does so by increasing the amount of evidence that a plaintiff must have before filing a lawsuit. In particular, the following three concepts apply (with text taken from the Act):

The complaint shall specify each statement alleged to have been misleading, the reason or reasons why the statement is misleading, and, if an allegation regarding the statement or omission is made on information and belief, the complaint shall state with particularity all facts on which that belief is formed.

The complaint shall, with respect to each act or omission alleged to violate this chapter, state with particularity facts giving rise to a strong inference that the defendant acted with the required state of mind. (Author's note: This means the defendant knew a statement was false at the time it was made, or was reckless in not recognizing that it was false)

The plaintiff shall have the burden of proving that the act or omission of the defendant alleged to violate this chapter (of the Act) caused the loss for which the plaintiff seeks to recover damages.

All of these concepts were designed to place a burden of proof on the plaintiff, requiring the presentation of substantial evidence before a judge would accept a case.

The Act also contains the following provisions, which make it less likely that a lawsuit will be converted into a class action lawsuit:

- The judge determines who is the most adequate plaintiff for a class action, which may not be the plaintiff that originally filed suit
- Investors must receive full disclosure of the terms of proposed settlements
- Favored plaintiffs cannot receive bonus payments

In short, the Act makes it more difficult for a plaintiff to file suit, for it is necessary to have evidence of fraudulent behavior without the discovery process (which is only allowed *after* the plaintiff has presented proof of fraud).

An additional provision of this Act, contained within Section 301, is that the auditor is required to report evidence of illegal activity to the client's board of directors, or the audit committee of the board of directors. The board or its audit committee is then obligated to notify the SEC of this notification within one business day. If the auditor does not receive a copy of the board's notification to the SEC within one business day, he or she is obliged to withdraw from the engagement and notify the SEC directly of the report previously made to the board. If the auditor does not do so, then the auditor may be subject to additional liabilities, including an assumption of fraud or collusion with the client. This is an unusual case in which the auditor is required to breach the normal obligation governing the confidentiality of client information.

Blue Sky Laws

The state governments individually enacted blue sky laws to prevent securities dealers from committing fraud through the sale of fake securities to investors. The "blue sky" name is derived from being able to "sell the sky" to an investor without the restrictions of any regulations. In essence, blue sky laws mandate that securities being offered for sale for the first time be qualified by the state regulatory commission, and registered with the state. Further, the terms and prices of the securities must follow the statutory guidelines imposed by the state. These guidelines are usually modeled on the Uniform Securities Act of 1956, for which the main provisions are:

- *Reason for existence.* The securities issuer is engaged in business. It is not bankrupt or in an organizational state, nor is it a blind pool, blank check, or shell company that has no purpose for being in existence.
- *Price.* The security is priced at a reasonable level in comparison to its current market price.
- *Unsold allotment.* The security is not related to any unsold allotments given to a securities dealer who has underwritten the security.
- *Asset base.* The issuer owns a minimum amount of assets.

An issuing entity is exempt from the blue sky laws if its securities are listed on a national stock exchange, such as the NASDAQ or New York Stock Exchange. For businesses listed in this manner, states issue a "manual exemption," which (despite the name) automatically allows securities to be sold within their borders. This exemption was initiated under the National Securities Markets Improvement Act of 1996.

The exemption is not so clear if an issuer's securities are only available for sale in the over the counter (OTC) market. If an issuer registers with one of the credit rating agencies and renews the registration each year, the majority of state governments will allow a registration exemption.

A plaintiff can be expected to use whichever of the preceding types of liability is expected to result in the best possible outcome. They may also combine several of these sources of liability into a single suit.

Client Losses Claimed as Damages

When a client brings suit against an auditor, the amount of damages claimed is based on the client's estimate of losses sustained. For example, if the auditor fails to spot a case of fraud, the client could claim damages in the amount of the losses it sustained from the fraud. Or, if the auditor prepared the client's annual tax return, the client could claim losses in the amount of any tax penalties incurred due to an improper filing.

Criminal Liability for Auditors

Of particular concern to the auditor is whether there are any situations in which criminal charges could be brought. There are two instances in which this is the case. Section 24 of the Securities Act of 1933 imposes the following penalties, which can include imprisonment of up to five years:

> Any person who willfully violates any of the provisions of this title, or the rules and regulations promulgated by the Commission under authority thereof, or any person who willfully, in a registration statement filed under this title, makes any untrue statement of a material fact or omits to state any material fact required to be stated therein or necessary to make the statements therein not misleading, shall upon conviction be fined not more than $10,000 or **imprisoned not more than five years**, or both.

In addition, Section 32(a) of the Securities Exchange Act of 1934 imposes the following penalties, which can include a substantially longer period of imprisonment:

> Any person who willfully violates any provision of this title... or any rule or regulation thereunder the violation of which is made unlawful or the observance of which is required under the terms of this title, or any person who willfully and knowingly makes, or causes to be made, any statement in any application, report, or document required to be filed under this title or any rule or regulation thereunder or undertaking contained in a registration statement... which statement was false or misleading with respect to any material fact, shall upon conviction be fined not more than $5,000,000, or **imprisoned not more than 20 years**, or both...

In short, there is a possibility that improperly-conducted audits of publicly-held clients can result in imprisonment for the auditor, as well as the much more common monetary damages.

SEC Actions Against Auditors

The Securities and Exchange Commission routinely reviews the financial statements of public companies, and can take action against those auditors who do not appear to be properly engaging in the public watchdog function. The SEC's cases against auditors generally fall into two categories, which are audit failures and auditor independence violations. An *audit failure* occurs when an auditor deviates from the applicable professional standards in such a way that indicates the opinion contained in its audit report is false. Audit failures are frequently associated with inadequate auditor training, failure to exercise sufficient professional skepticism in evaluating management representations, not sufficiently evaluating client valuation estimates, essentially not engaging in any auditing activities at all, and/or creating inadequate audit documentation.

As for independence, an auditor must be independent of its clients, both in appearance and in fact. The SEC has recently brought cases against auditors in the following independence-related areas:

- Providing bookkeeping and expert services to affiliates of audit clients
- Auditing personnel owning stock in audit clients or affiliates of audit clients
- Lobbying on behalf of audit clients
- Service by audit firm employees on the boards of audit clients
- Close personal relationships between senior management at audit clients and senior engagement personnel

For example, the SEC has censured several audit firms for a lack of independence following audit firm mergers, when several partners and other audit professionals held investments in the securities of firm audit clients. Other independence-related censures have involved auditors engaging in business relationships with their audit clients.

The SEC uses its Rule 102(e) of the Commission's Rules of Practice to ensure auditor accountability. The Rule allows the SEC to censure, or permanently or temporarily deny auditors the privilege of appearing or practicing before the SEC if they are found by the SEC to have engaged in improper professional conduct. Improper professional conduct includes reckless conduct, a single act of highly unreasonable conduct in circumstances warranting heightened scrutiny, or repeated instances of unreasonable conduct that indicates a lack of competence. Some of the actions taken by the SEC against auditors include the following:

- Suspension from accepting audit engagements from new SEC registrants for a period of time.
- Suspension with a right to apply for reinstatement after a period of time.
- Retention of an independent consultant to work with the auditor to assure that the auditor implements policies and procedures that can be expected to remedy independence violations.
- Suspensions from practice for specified audit partners.
- Monetary settlements payable to the government.

A key element of SEC actions is the *consent decree*, which is an order based upon an agreement between the parties, instead of continuing the case through a trial or hearing. A consent decree is almost always final and non-appealable. Consent decrees are common practice when the government has sued to make a person or entity comply with the law.

REAL-LIFE SEC ACTION

A case of SEC action against an audit firm is the 2019 case involving KPMG LLP. The SEC charged KPMG with altering past audit work after illegally obtaining confidential information from the Public Company Accounting Oversight Board (PCAOB). Several KPMG executives and audit partners conspired to obtain and use leaked PCAOB inspection plans in order to improve the firm's inspection results. This misconduct occurred between 2015 and 2017 and involved efforts to revise audit documentation before PCAOB inspections took place.

The SEC found that KPMG not only violated audit integrity standards but also failed to maintain appropriate ethical controls. As a result, the firm agreed to pay a $50 million penalty and implement extensive remedial measures, including improved compliance training and internal controls. Additionally, several former KPMG officials faced criminal charges and were barred from practicing before the SEC.

PCAOB Actions Against Auditors

The Public Company Accounting Oversight Board (PCAOB) oversees the audits of publicly-held companies. It does so by overseeing the qualifications and activities of the audit firms that engage in public company audits, and can impose discipline on these firms. By imposing a high level of discipline on auditors, it is thought that the

PCAOB can minimize the risk of not finding material financial statement errors, thereby protecting investors.

The PCAOB has the authority to investigate and discipline registered public accounting firms and persons associated with those firms for noncompliance with the Sarbanes-Oxley Act of 2002, the rules of the PCAOB and the SEC, and other laws, rules, and professional standards governing the audits of public companies, brokers, and dealers. When violations are found, the PCAOB can impose sanctions, and can also discipline auditors who fail to cooperate with its investigations.

A range of sanctions may be imposed, including censure, monetary penalties, revocation of a firm's registration with the PCAOB, and a ban on an individual's association with registered accounting firms.

REAL-LIFE PCAOB ACTION

An example of a PCAOB action against an audit firm is the 2023 disciplinary action against KPMG Korea. The PCAOB sanctioned the firm for widespread quality control failures and violations of auditing standards related to multiple public company audits between 2016 and 2018.

The investigation revealed that KPMG Korea failed to properly supervise audits, allowed inadequate audit documentation, and did not sufficiently test key financial assertions. Additionally, the PCAOB found that the firm's system of quality control was not reasonably designed to provide reasonable assurance of compliance with professional standards. This included shortcomings in engagement performance, monitoring, and leadership responsibilities.

As a result, the PCAOB imposed a $350,000 civil penalty on KPMG Korea. Two partners involved in the audits were also sanctioned—one was barred from associating with a registered firm, and another was fined and given practice limitations.

Due Professional Care

Thus, far, we have described a picture for the auditor that appears to be decidedly grim. To defend against this plethora of lawsuits, the auditor can rely upon the concept of due professional care. *Due professional care* is exercised when audits are carried out in accordance with the standards set for the profession. The auditor is usually obligated to exercise due professional care by the terms of the engagement letter; the obligation exists even if it is not specifically stated in the engagement letter.

Proving that an auditor has exercised due professional care constitutes a complete defense against any charge brought by a plaintiff. This proof constitutes the bulk of the work in defending against lawsuits. Unfortunately for the auditor, proving one's case can be difficult when subsequent events turn out to be worse than the auditor could have expected, in which case the defense needs to also address the issue of whether the auditor should have seen a future event coming.

The due professional care concept may also be employed by the plaintiff. To prove the liability of an auditor, the plaintiff needs to prove that the auditor accepted the duty of due professional care (for which the evidence is the engagement letter) and was negligent, while the client suffered losses that were caused by the negligence of the auditor. A key element in this argument is causation, where the plaintiff has the burden of proving that the auditor's actions caused the losses incurred by the client. There may be cases in which the auditor can be proven to be negligent in an audit, and yet will not be found liable, because the negligent activity did not cause the loss suffered by the client.

The plaintiff will try to prove that the auditor breached his or her duty by showing that either the obligations stated in the engagement letter were not performed at all, or that they were performed at an inadequate level. Examples of these situations are:

- The auditor did not complete the audit by the agreed-upon time.
- The auditor did not detect an existing case of fraud within the client entity.

It is not possible to design a cost-effective audit that is assured of finding every misstatement that is due to client errors or fraud, since doing so would require a 100% review of all client records, which would be prohibitively expensive. Instead, the objective is to obtain reasonable assurance that these misstatements have been found; reaching a reasonable level of assurance is achieved by exercising due professional care.

The Contributory and Comparative Negligence Defenses

A reasonable defense for the auditor is *contributory negligence*, where the plaintiff did not act prudently, typically resulting in a situation where its actions or lack of actions contributed to the losses it suffered. Depending on state law, this defense may absolve the auditor of any guilt, or may just reduce the amount of any awards granted to the plaintiff.

EXAMPLE

Multiple members of senior management are actively participating in the shipment of empty boxes to customers in order to falsely increase the amount of reported sales. The auditor fails to spot the inflated sales. After the situation is revealed months later, the client sues the auditor for negligence in not spotting the fraud. A possible defense for the auditor is contributory negligence, where the client was contributing to the fraud, and so is also culpable in the situation.

A variation on the concept is *comparative negligence*, where the jury apportions blame among the various parties to the suit, including the plaintiff, based on causation. Damages are then allocated to each of the parties, based on the extent to which each one was at fault.

EXAMPLE

A jury finds that management and the auditor were each 50% at fault for not finding a case of fraud within the client, and so apportions the $100,000 losses suffered by the client between the two parties. This means that the client must absorb $50,000 of the losses that it suffered.

Yet another variation is *joint and several* liability, which arises when there is an obligation that can be enforced against a group of parties or against them individually.

EXAMPLE

A jury apportions a $1,000,000 judgment 20% to the client, 30% to the auditor, and 50% to three other parties. The other three parties are bankrupt and so cannot pay their share of the damages. Under the joint and several liability concept, the plaintiff can not only obtain the 30% due from the auditor, but can also collect from the auditor the other 50% that the co-defendants cannot afford to pay.

The *joint and proportionate* liability could be applied to a case. Under this concept, if some defendants are unable to pay their share of a judgment, the auditor's share increases proportionately. In those cases in which no other defendants can pay their fair share, the auditor will be liable for the entire amount of a judgment.

EXAMPLE

A jury apportions a $5 million judgment 30% to the auditor, 20% to an appraiser, and 50% to several other parties. This means that the auditor is liable for $1.5 million of the total judgment. However, the appraiser is unable to pay its $1 million share of the judgment, so this amount is apportioned among the remaining defendants. Based on its share of the judgment, the auditor must pay an additional $375,000.

The Other Causes Defense

Another possible defense for the auditor is that the losses suffered by the plaintiff were due to other causes than the actions of the auditor. There may be entirely different issues that triggered the loss, and which would have happened irrespective of any negligence by the auditor.

Professional Liability Insurance

Auditors routinely pay for professional liability insurance, which protects against claims that services provided to a client caused the client to suffer financial harm due to mistakes on the part of the auditor, or because the auditor failed to perform some service. This insurance covers any losses awarded to plaintiffs, up to a certain maximum amount. It can also cover the cost of defending the auditor in a civil lawsuit, even if the legal action turns out to be groundless. However, some awarded claims are so large that they exceed the amount of the insurance, which means that any residual must be paid by the audit firm. In addition, this insurance comes with a large deductible, so an auditor will be self-insuring against a portion of any losses that may be incurred.

The cost of professional liability insurance continues to increase at a rapid rate, because it can be quite expensive to defend a lawsuit, even when the price charged by the auditor for an audit engagement is quite low. It is not unheard of for the cost of a legal defense to exceed the related audit fee by a factor of well over 100.

Auditor Risk Mitigation

There are a number of steps that auditors can take to reduce their legal liability. Consider the following alternatives:

- *Professional liability insurance.* Always maintain an adequate level of professional liability insurance coverage, and regularly review the amount of coverage to ensure that it reflects changes in the auditor's client base.
- *Client investigation.* Always conduct a thorough investigation of prospective clients to see if there have been any prior allegations of impropriety against client management or the company as a whole. The departure of a prior auditor from an engagement with the prospective client is another warning sign, as is the presence of significant transactions with related parties. It may not be worthwhile to ever work for a prospective client that is experiencing financial difficulties, since its investors and creditors will be quite likely to pursue the auditor for monetary satisfaction if the client goes bankrupt.
- *Engagement letters.* Never begin an engagement without both parties first signing off on a written engagement letter. Otherwise, the client may not have a clear understanding of the services to be provided, which can lead to the filing of a lawsuit. Depending on the situation, it may also be possible to include an indemnification or hold harmless clause in the letter, perhaps in relation to any knowing misrepresentations by management.
- *Report boilerplate.* Always include in financial statements the exact wording provided in the *Statements on Auditing Standards* and the *Statements on Standards for Accounting and Review Services*, which state the nature of the services provided and the extent of the responsibility being assumed by the auditor.
- *Capacity and competence.* Before engaging with an audit client, verify that the firm and its assigned personnel have sufficient capacity and competence to audit the client in accordance with professional standards.
- *Understanding of the client.* Block out a sufficient amount of time to obtain a reasonably deep understanding of the client's business, as well as any unusual industry practices that may apply to the client.
- *Planning and execution.* Audits must be properly planned and executed, including the identification of significant risks that are then addressed through

adequate audit procedures. The auditor must be careful to comply with all generally accepted auditing standards.

- *Internal control analysis.* Be particularly careful to assess the risk of errors and fraud when there are material weaknesses in a client's system of internal controls.
- *Professional skepticism.* The auditor must exercise appropriate professional skepticism, gather sufficient audit evidence, adequately document completed tasks, and require more sufficient evidential matter than simple representations from management.
- *Consult internally.* When troublesome issues arise, have knowledgeable people available to assist in sensitive areas. In addition, auditors must be willing to push back against obstreperous clients when their concerns are not addressed.
- *Independence.* Auditors must have robust monitoring processes and training on independence issues, in order to comply with independence requirements. Many independence-related issues can be avoided through strong processes, as well as a tone at the top that emphasizes auditor independence.
- *Non-audit engagements.* Always exercise due professional care when performing compilation or review services, which includes following up on clearly unusual or missing items. Otherwise, a client could sue on the grounds of negligence.
- *Legal counsel.* Retain legal counsel in order to discuss all client situations that could lead to legal liability. Consider the attorney's advice regarding how to mitigate or avoid any identified risks.

Summary

The auditor is subject to significant legal liabilities, especially when work is performed for publicly-held clients. Significant points related to auditor legal liability are:

- The auditor is liable for any failure to exercise due professional care.
- The auditor can be liable to third parties who use the financial statements of a client, usually including anyone who can be foreseen to be a user of a client's financial statements.
- The federal securities laws impose a higher degree of liability on the auditor, to include the buyers and sellers of a client's securities.
- There are limited situations in which an auditor can be held criminally liable if the audit of a public entity was improperly conducted.

To mitigate the risk of legal liability, there are a number of policies and procedures that an auditor can implement to keep from working with at-risk clients and conduct audits at a high standard of excellence. Finally, to guard against a judgement against the auditor, always have an adequate amount of professional liability insurance.

Glossary

A

Audit failure. When an auditor deviates from the applicable professional standards in such a way that indicates the opinion contained in its audit report is false.

C

Common law. Law that has been developed over time through a series of court decisions.

Comparative negligence. A method for allocating damages among negligent parties based on the degree to which each one was at fault.

Consent decree. An order based upon an agreement between the parties, instead of continuing the case through a trial or hearing.

Contributory negligence. Negligence by the plaintiff that contributed to the loss incurred.

D

Due professional care. A level of work that is exercised when audits are carried out in accordance with the standards set for the profession.

E

Engagement letter. A letter between an auditor and a client that sets forth the relationship between the parties.

F

Fraud. The misrepresentation of a material fact, with the intent to deceive the other party.

G

Gross negligence. The reckless disregard for one's professional responsibilities.

J

Joint and several liability. When there is an obligation that can be enforced against a group or against them individually.

N

Negligence. The breach of one's duty, resulting in loss or injury.

P

Plaintiff. The party bringing suit against a defendant.

Proportionate liability. A method for allocating damages among negligent parties, where each entity is liable according to its pro rata share of any damages awarded to the plaintiff.

R

Registration statement. A document submitted to the Securities and Exchange Commission when a company wants to sell securities to the public.

S

Statutory law. Law that has been issued by federal or state legislative bodies.

Index

www.ingramcontent.com/pod-product-compliance
Lightning Source LLC
Chambersburg PA
CBHW051432200326
41520CB00023B/7445